Poetry & Verse
of the Beloved

Poetry & Verse of the Beloved

Poetry and artwork by Jane Gibbs, the author of The Company of Laid Down Lovers

Dedication

All for you my beloved King

ISBN-13:9798357722539
Editing: Mary King
Cover design: Jane Gibbs
Cover Artwork: 'The Secret Garden' by Jane Gibbs
Internal artwork: Jane Gibbs
Publisher: Jane Gibbs KDP Publishing Services

'Frequency' The Ruah breath of God; the living breath of God; His voice speaking out.

This was painted during a time of prayer during the global pandemic. I believe this was His answer. His frequency coming to a world in trouble.

As poets and artists arise to bring glory, hope, and love we are part of the frequency of God.

THE SOUND IS LOVE!

Acknowledgements

It is with much gratitude that I acknowledge the many people who have spoken into my life and cheered me on throughout enabling me to reach this point. Especially my sisters and fellow founding members of 'Liz Wright's International Mentoring Community'. I am so thankful for the way that each of you have loved me and seen the treasures that God has stored within, calling them forth and championing me to excel. I love the Jesus in every one of you and the bridal walk we are all on together.

I would also like to thank my husband and beautiful children that have loved and supported me throughout the process of endless painting sessions and hours of typing, scribbling, and recording poetry as the inspiration came. With particular appreciation to Riley Gibbs, also a poet, for the encouragement and sometimes brutal honesty to help hone my skill as I found my poetic voice.

Mary King as always what an asset you are! Such a beautiful woman of God, your expertise and professionalism is astounding. I couldn't have done this without your help.

Lastly I want to express my heartfelt thanks to Julie Brown, you are such a great inspiration. Always encouraging, supportive and capable of easing us all out of our comfort zones with such gentle care. I am honoured to call you friend.

Endorsements

"It is my joy to commend this beautiful expression of poetry and art to you. In Jane's unique style, spiritual encounters and God experiences are carefully crafted with inspiring words and pictures inviting the reader to reflect and open up to the deep ways of The Father and the gentle nudges of His Spirit. You will be refreshed and revived towards your true identity and destiny, without doubt. Such an opportunity in our hands - well done and thank you Jane!"

Jenny Watson
Kingdom Advance Network
Apostolic Leader, Author, and Coach

"Jane Gibbs has the gift of bringing the reader into the heart of the Lord. As you read this book, you will be captivated by the words that are so eloquently penned, which will bring you into the place of oneness with God. Jane is a gifted writer who has tapped into the Bridal Chamber of God in which you will be ushered into the place of becoming consumed by His heart and His love. This book is one that should be savored, cherished, and could be used in a small group that would help to lead each reader into a deeper relationship and intimacy with Him."

Stephanie Claiborne
Founder of Heart of Gold Ministries International and Fullness of Joy, LLC
Author of Fullness of Joy

Foreword

"So much beauty flows from this sacred book, 'Poetry & Verse of the Beloved'. A very special collection of poetry and artwork, Jane's writing allows us to open the gate of her heart and enter in, for just a while, to the secret garden of her relationship with Jesus.

In three volumes, the poems flow like the sparkling brook Jane so often describes a source of life-giving water to drink from, refreshing and revitalising the heart. The themes of each poem speak gently and yet powerfully, beautiful language capturing Jane's inward journey with her King.

Now and again, as I lingered through the pages, Jesus surprised me. He met me where I was unaware of my need for him and, as the pages turned, His Presence reached ever deeper. Jane's writing is alive with the breath of the Spirit, speaking the truth and through each word one hears His invitation, "Come away with Me." It touched me deeply to sense his involvement in Jane's life and His love for this beautiful book.

Beautiful, original artwork intersperses the poetry, providing moments to pause, to admire and appreciate the gift God has given to the artist, to drink in the fathomless love of our God. This book is so sensitively and beautifully arranged.

As the Bride awakens, now we can turn to works such as these, seeing them as sovereign gifts for our journey, to strengthen, inspire and show the way. I see Jane's book as one of the first fruits of the new fruit Jesus is releasing in our generation. It is a work that will endure for all time."

Julie Brown
Author & Founder of The Proverbs 31 Movement

Contents

Part Two – True Identity

Part Three – The Intimate Poet

Introduction

My first book, 'The Company of Laid Down Lovers', came from my soul journey in Christ and how by yielding my life and surrendering my heart to Jesus, I was able to love myself and others. I learnt to love from the God of love! It is from that place that I poured out my heart onto the page in poetry and expressed my journey and His prophetic voice over my life on the canvas.

This collection of poetry and artwork is presented in three parts: Life's Journey, True Identity and The Intimate Poet.

I hope that this book will draw you deeper into the heart of a loving God as you allow Him in.

Listen for Him as He knocks on the door of your heart.

Part One
Life's Journey

Foreword

This section is compiled of poems that describe my internal journey over the years. From a frantic, chaotic heart to a place of restful bliss.

As I found my place inside of God's heart, I learnt to love myself just as I am. I began to learn from my mistakes and failings instead of lamenting them. I also grew in my ability to let go of my old behaviour patterns and learnt to trust myself and the Lord as I surrendered to Him.

This journey starts with holding offence and ends with understanding my destiny in Christ.

OFFENCE IN MY HEART

I opened the door and allowed offence into my heart!

It caused a splinter, a fracture, and left a jagged edge.

This caused me pain.

It was left unchecked, and I bled.

I bled out disquiet and dislike until no hope or peace was left.

So I closed the door; masked it with false love

And hid it away under politeness and well-rehearsed good manners.

But in the dark, it was festering—disregarded, neglected and forgotten.

Every now and then, it would speak out, its voice trying to be heard.

And then you came, Holy Spirit, with your surgeon's knife.

The anaesthetic used was unconditional love and total acceptance.

You said, "This offence does not belong in the heart of a child of God".

And so, as I surrendered and trusted you,

You removed the offence from my heart and healed the wound,

Sealing and cauterising the wound with your love.

The offence was removed, and the wound healed.

'A New Day' is the overcoming of a difficult season and speaks of life and hope. There is a lot of energy, life, and vibrancy on a restful, light background.

FOR HE KNOWS THE PLANS HE HAS FOR ME

The Holy Spirit shows me the way,

He leads me to the door of the Father's house.

He reminds me to bring all the places of my heart.

He encourages me to go with Him, not to falter or delay.

The Father is waiting.

I arrive at the door and Jesus meets me there.

He says, "Did you bring it?

Father is waiting for you, beloved one".

I look puzzled, and He smiles and goes on to explain,

"That secret prayer, the silent one.

When you were confused, angry, scared or alone.

The times you felt let down or unheard.

When He didn't answer.

That moment!

You thought He hadn't noticed but Father heard it all.

He is waiting to discuss it now.

He wants to look you in the eyes with love, and let you know the truth".

(Continued....)

I arrive and stand before the Father, less confident than before

But then a boldness fills me, and I speak more than a whisper.

No silent prayer today!

I ask,

"Why Father?"

And a sadness flickers across His beautiful face.

I say, "Where were you?"

And a tear rolls down His cheek.

"How could you leave me at that moment?

Where were your promises?", I challenge.

He speaks, and so much amazing love is in His voice.

"I have you, precious one. I always did.

Those tiny moments are so small and the plans I have for you are so wide".

"Look!", He directs.

I see the glorious promise of He and I in eternity.

I say, "Who are all the others?".

He smiles; His intense, passionate love over me, His child.

"Those are the lives you touched on your way to finding me

In every impossible moment and place of pain.

Your pursuit, your questions, brought them to me too.

So you see, the plans I have for you are not just about you".

He's Got This

I collapse before the Father,

Still waiting for the promise.

Delivery date soon,

Physical manifestation to come.

But I am tired!

Hoping is exhausting

When it comes from my flesh.

My spirit knows and she rejoices,

But me—I have moments of weariness!

"Did God actually say?", echoes in my mind.

But He is faithful, forever true,

Ever good, and always kind.

"Is this true?

So where are you now, Father?".

He comes very close, and whispers calm and clear,

"I'm here," He says, "I got this!

I really have, it's in my hands.

There's nothing more for you to do, weary or rejoicing,

you choose. It's up to you.

It's your journey, child, but I tell you this,

I have the world within my hands, I've really have got this".

He takes my hand in His hand.

I stand unsteady on my feet and let Him lead.

Now I know He's got this, So I surrender as I rest within His peace.

STONES FOR LIVING BREAD

"Why carry these stones?", I hear you enquire.

"It's all I have to sustain me," is my clipped reply,

"I've collected them all from over the years:

Old wives' tales and legends, sayings, and stories".

"These will not feed you; they won't give you life.

They will not restore you; you will not be revived.

They will not give you strength or the power you need,

So let go of these stones and return here to Me.

Do you not know? Have you not heard?

You'll be fed from the words from my mouth,

For I am your Lord".

So I returned to the book, the Word of our God.

I used fresh understanding as I looked at the truth.

No more to remember the old religion or rules,

But for wisdom I prayed as I enquired of my Lord.

Then I saw you right here, in the midst of the pages

As I read of your story down through the ages—

The love of a Saviour, a Father and Friend.

I saw destiny, purpose, the beginning, and end.

I looked to my hands; it was then that I saw

Fresh manna from heaven and a past now restored.

I began to believe there was more than I'd seen

As unrolled before me a gold path at my feet.

My glorious future, right before me unfolded,

So much bigger and brighter than what I'd been told.

Now I have chosen to read with eyes that see life,

Not rules or religion but a tale of a King and His wife.

This is truly good news! No more stones now for me.

Fresh bread, a bright hope in my found destiny.

LIKE THE BROOK

"Peace be still!",

were the words from you. You described it thus,

"A gentle, babbling brook, winding its way forward.

A gentle flow, staying the course—not a torrent or cascade!"

You speak of this,

"A brook or a stream knows its course. Its destination remains true.

It does not rush or hurry and neither should you.

It still sustains life and reaches its destiny.

Its purpose fulfilled by the Creator's intentionality.

It still moves onward and sings its sweet song.

The light glistens on its edge as it ambles along.

For it knows it will torrent and its pace will quicken soon

But for now, it will trickle and tumble along.

One thing in its purpose, in this season it brings,

A peace and a rest, as its quiet song it sings."

So rest, child of God, and go with the Spirit's flow

For it's His peace He is building as forward, you go.

For He knows of your frailty and the ardent path ahead,

So rest in this season and be gently led.

THE LOCKED DOOR

It was locked from the inside
And I held the key.
No one was to enter this dark part of me.
I hadn't ventured for so long,
The lock was rusty, stiff, and old.
The part of me locked inside
Was afraid, alone, and cold.
Yet His fervent whispers
And His passion caused a stir.
I relinquished the key I held
So that He could go to her.

Enfolded

I rest and we laugh together, my Lover and I,
For we know the pure joy of 'perfect'.
This perfect love that drives out all former loves
and melts the icy pain of former torment,
Fears, betrayals, and hope deferred.
I am free to live in the internal embrace.
He and I smile at the knowledge that I am held.
No past tie can hold me when I am here,
And no mindset is higher than His truth.
So, I allow the washing in His pure light.
The darkness is extinguished, and any torment flees in fear
As the Perfect Lover sings His passion for my soul, over and over.
For I am held in here!

Now, if anyone is enfolded into Christ, he has become an entirely new person.
All that is related to the old order has vanished. Behold, everything is fresh and new.

2 Corinthians 5:17 (TPT)

ONE STEP AT A TIME

So, it dawned on me, one day on my climb.

As I face my mountain, It's one step at a time!

I look up and see those eyes always on me

I stare in surprise—

He's laughing at me as I realise

My mountain is one step at a time.

I would if I could, cast this mount to the sea.

He says I could, but what of discovery?

How else would I learn then, on my journey?

My muscles are strong, and the outlook is fine.

I've grown so much on this mountain of mine.

Look how far I have travelled and who I've become

Because I chose to win my battle and follow the Son.

So, He looks for my gaze and holds out His Hand.

I smile and I laugh as I stumble, then stand.

Step after step, I follow His climb,

My feet pushing forward one step at a time.

'*Sacred Waterfall*' symbolises where I imagine myself to be when I am alone with the Lord; the water tumbling down over flint-like rocks and the musical sound of the cascading splashes.

The Still Waters

I have found my way here to this place.

The tumble of the waterfall causes the rocks to shimmer and glow.

The stream bubbles and froths as the water dances and sprays.

I move along the bank to where the stream quietly flows.

Its lullaby sings, "Peace, be still". I stop.

It's here I see Him, in our secret space—our spot.

He is leaning by our tree which gives us shelter and shade.

The sweet scent of blossoming love, drawing me in so enticingly.

He smiles and love spreads across His radiant face.

I stand before Him, beholding and regarding my King.

Hot liquid-love fills and melts me.

I dissolve in it, drowning in its intensity.

His eyes speak of acceptance, approval and more.

As He reaches to touch the deep places in my inner parts with just a look,

Overwhelmed by His passion and jealous eyes, I hit the floor.

I fall at His feet, my worship and adoration bubbling out like the brook.

I am overwhelmed in this moment.

It's just us. Our moment!

(Continued....)

He moves to sit under the tree, and I lay my head on His chest
As He strokes away the burdens and the worries from my brow.
There are no clocks or deadlines, burdens, or cares, and I rest.
He sings the ancient ballad prepared, so sweet and low.

The song of a Man who was God and became a sacrifice,
Longing for His love, with His life He paid the price.

He sings of a girl who was lost and found by a King.
Such a beautiful song as these truths fill the air,
I rest in this peaceful spot, just me here with Him.
He brings peace and hope in the place of my cares.

I arise, feeling stronger as His love pulsates through my veins.
I know I must move from here but vow to come again.

I lock this memory in my heart, a treasure to keep.
"I need to go", I whisper. "I'll come with you", He smiles.
We walk hand in hand, past the singing waterfall so sweet.
I slow my pace as we leave, desperate to linger awhile.

The water song is fading, the sun's rays no longer on our backs.
I am sitting in my room, my Bible open on my lap.

I know He is with me, in the silence of my room.
"I will go back again", I say aloud in resolve.
"I know", He replies, and we both hope that it's soon.
"I will meet you there", He whispers into the depths of my soul.

WHEN GOD BREATHES

When the Lord breathes into me, then I have breath again.

When God blows into my heart, my dying embers become a flame.

"Reignite my passion, Lord", I ask Almighty God, my King.

"Blow into the dead parts of my soul, that I may live again".

Parts crushed by disappointment, squashed by trauma, killed by sin.

Places starved of love and kindness; I bring these now to Him.

"Breathe your life, Lord. Let me live. Let my embers catch ablaze

That I may burn again with purpose, to set on fire in your name.

Let me reveal your character resurrected, set on fire,

Every part of me alive again; living for you, my desire!"

A FRESH REVELATION

And so, it comes like a thief in the night,

So unexpected, stopping me in my tracks.

The sense of your presence and a dawning realisation,

I KNOW WHAT I DIDN'T KNOW BEFORE.

I remember asking, searching, seeking you out.

No understanding. In the dark!

I understand and it all makes sense,

I KNOW YOU BETTER THAN I DID BEFORE

I'm wiser now, there's clarity.

I have understanding. The penny's dropped!

We smile at each other as I confess,

"I KNOW WHAT I DIDN'T KNOW BEFORE!"

Surrender

I choose His feet and I kneel,
Every chamber of my heart, Spirit-filled.
I incline my ear to hear His voice, sweet and divine.
I gaze in the hope His eyes catch mine.
What a glorious surrender!
A love-sacrifice.
No hurry to leave as I rest in this place,
Our eyes locked as you speak within.
I am wholly yours, my Bridegroom King.

The Path to Humility

(Taken from 'The Company of Laid Down Lovers' J Gibbs 2021)

The path to humility

Is more of Him and less of me.

To come and bow before His throne,

To make this place my only home.

To surrender and listen at His feet,

To hear His voice, so strong and sweet.

To empty myself of me and mine,

And to be filled with His love divine.

To embrace in Him, my true identity

And to clothe myself in His humility.

The path is not to beat up my heart,

Nor to crucify again my darker parts,

But sweet surrender and relinquished control,

And give to Him my heart and soul.

To say, "Yes and amen" to His voice,

And in my lowliness, rejoice.

And so I choose this path to Him,

To prostrate myself before the King.

Jane Gibbs

'Ascending Glory' From a place of humility, we can ascend in glory. As we choose to bow low at the feet of Jesus, so we shall be lifted up to see the glorious, breathtaking view in the heavenly places.

Jane Gibbs

'Horizon' The deepness of the majestic purple, depicts our royalty as co-heirs of Christ. As we yield to the vastness of His glory and pursue the height and hiddenness of God in the secret place, so we see revelation light on the horizon!

I Yield

I choose to yield to the passionate embrace

And abandon myself to His affectionate kiss.

I say, "Yes" to His zealous pursuit of my being

And submit to that jealous love that calls me to Him.

I yield to His song that sings to my wandering heart.

I tender my surrender to His wooing, lyrical stanza.

He woos my heart and calls me back to Himself as my King.

He sings me back to life and loves me back to loving Him.

I am His and He is mine.

My one true love, our hearts entwined.

So I yield and say, "Yes", for He has won.

I relinquish all, for I am undone.

'The Mountain Top' I painted this during a turbulent time in the world. This is my divine space, the mountain top with God. Here, the air is clear and bright, and I can gain His perspective.

THE HOLY MOUNTAIN

(Inspired by Song of Songs Chapter 4)

He calls me to go with Him and gives me His hand.
Our fingers interlace and lend me His strength as we climb.
I cannot see the top so I focus on His face, with our fingers entwined.
His voice ignites fire and excitement within my heart.
I do not know the way, yet He leads me on this ancient path.
The aroma of our union saturates this space.
I breathe in such a sweet scent of this fragrant place.
It is our love: His sacrifice and my surrendered heart.

I could stay here forever in this blissful peace,
Yet He urges me onward and higher we climb.
"There's more", is spoken within me, resounding in my spirit.
I hold tightly, leaning into Him, His hand holding mine.
I see the fruitful vineyards in the valley below,
Further up I see the eagles soar as they shriek their love for the King
For they know where we go.

But now I see nothing, for the cloud becomes thick and heavy
With such an awesome mist and terrifying glory.
I falter, for the fear of the Lord grips my inner man.
"How can I go on?" I cry, "This is no place for me".
Yet my King holds on tighter and says, "Come. Come with me".
I am restored as I see His shining eyes, His face full of perfect love.
And so, I persist on this fearsome journey above.

We are here, in this glorious, swirling mist near to the throne—
Flashes of fire and perfect holiness. I am undone.
I fall on my face, crying out at the majesty of the King.
The awe and wonder of my God takes over my fallible heart
As I hear the resounding glory rise up in the heavens and I take my part.
He covers me with His humility and pure innocence as I simply worship Him.
To the altar before me, I bring my offering.
It is His sacrifice and my surrendered heart.

'Divine Destiny' was painted during a live worship session on New Year's Day, 2021. It portrays the new season after the difficulties endured by so many people. There is so much colour and texture, and a clear pathway ahead. Although the destination is not seen, the journey is full of light and colour.

*D*ivine *D*estiny

I find my place in His heart

As He resides in mine.

I find I am in the centre of His will

When He is in the centre of mine.

Every moment of the day, He waits for my gaze.

Every breath, an opportunity to speak His name.

Every flutter of my eye, a chance to seek His face

And gaze into the eyes that gaze into mine.

No rules or control but compelling love.

To know and be known by my King above.

And now I incline my ear as I hear Him call to me.

To live with the walls of Him is my divine destiny.

Part Two
True Identity

Foreword

Personally, I have found that as I allowed Christ to take centre stage in my life, I began to listen to how He described me. I did this through reading the Word of God (the Bible) from a position of understanding a God of love who desired a relationship with my heart, rather than as a text of rules and rituals.

I experienced many precious encounters, both from sitting with the Lord in prayer, during times of worship and studying the text in the Word of God. I kept my heart open and available, and readily listened to what the Holy Spirit whispered within.

There were arguments, battles, and tears, but ultimately, it led to victorious peace and a defined understanding of my true self.

My identity is that I am a surrendered bride, a beautiful creation made in God's image. I am purposed for relationship with Him and am a conduit of God's immense love for His world.

'Internal Beauty' celebrates beauty and symbolises the choice to value our inner beauty. It is from this place that we mature and flourish as our true selves.

Hello Me!

What do I see when I unlock the door—

Behind the eyes, beneath the skin, as I look to the core?

Not my reflection in a mirror or another's speech,

Not an opinion formed or judgement reached,

Not tall, not short, not fat, or thin.

Who is this creature housed within?

I know what I like and what makes me cry,

I remember dreams and hopes of a lifetime gone by.

My manners and duties, expectations, and roles,

As I wear many hats for the people I know.

But as I sit here, just me with my thoughts looking in,

I see her emerging, the princess within.

"Hello me", I say, "let's chat for a while".

"It's been so long", I remark with a smile.

"Do you know you are loved by me, and others too?

There you are friend. So, how are you?".

Independent Spirit

Independent spirit, it's time to say goodbye.

I value how you have helped me in the journey of my life.

You gave me strength when I was weak

And courage in the face of fear.

But that time has passed now, and I must leave you here.

In you I had determination to go forward,

And answers when there were none.

When I felt hopeless against the storm,

In you is where I felt strong.

But now I have a new ally,

One who is bigger and stronger than you.

He is my strength and courage

And my vision to see it through.

He leads me by still waters,

And helps me stand against the storm.

And in the weariness of battle,

It is He that leads me home.

His wisdom is my answer,

His understanding forms my plans.

He calls for my surrender as He holds out His hands.

He was there from the beginning and celebrates my victorious end.

He is the Holy Spirit, my Mentor, Helper, Friend.

JUST BE

Today before the Father, this was my plea,

"Can I have the space for me to be me?".

My glorious, faithful Father replied,

"I have given you my permission, my beautiful child.

You, my beloved, have all the space in my heart.

It's your own permission you need for you to start

To give yourself space, to let go of you,

To relinquish contending and pushing through.

Choose to let go and relax into me,

To snuggle in tight—it's time to be free.

I love the way that you hold my gaze

Just by being the one uniquely made.

My creation, my delight, see who I see

So let go of all your standards and just be free".

Many Hats

In my life I wear many hats: Friend, Mother, Wife.

But before you, I am just myself,

Offering up my heart, my life.

My only role, to respond in love

With my own love in return,

To stand before the altar

And allow my love to burn.

In life I have many roles, routines, to-do lists and more

But when I enter the secret place,

It's just my presence you adore.

Sometimes I wash your feet with my tears,

Other times I worship you and sing.

You always cherish these special times

And embrace all that I bring.

So because of these hidden moments,

I can walk through life with grace

As others smell your fragrance

And see your reflection in my face.

*W*ilderness *W*ithin

He meets me in the wilderness of my heart,

Right in the place of bitter pain and old strife.

The door was locked. A private place;

Neglected, overgrown and barren of life.

Why here—

There is nothing for my Lord here?

Only empty regrets and resentments,

Yet He draws near.

He seems unaffected by what I have hidden.

He makes no excuses for arriving unbidden.

What about my success? Or where my heart loves you best?

On the moments of glory, choose there, Lord to rest.

Yet He chooses this barren spot,

Devoid of life, no holiness or goodness here.

Just the raw ache of a forgotten wound of envy, anger, and fear.

He is not fazed by the unpleasant stench,

For He died for this part of my heart.

His blood washes the ground and He speaks healing and peace.

He calls for my surrender, my heart, and brings me release.   (Continued....)

It is here that He asks me to relinquish my pain

As He whispers new life and restores once again.

He brings me His strength, "Get up now", He commands.

I stand to my feet and rest in His arms.

I hold to Him tightly as unsteadily I walk.

Nothing is said, no reason to talk!

As He gracefully leads me away from this place,

I receive joy and His peace as I look to His face.

Now I lean upon Him with each step as we leave,

A new space within me for His love and grace to weave.

I lean on my Lover, my wilderness gone,

Another part of my heart restored with His song.

'Breathe' shows a garden in close up. Sometimes our hearts can look wild and unruly internally, yet beautiful to the observer. Others witness the flowers growing and the breeze moving their heads, releasing the fragrance. They may not notice what we perceive to be our unruly undergrowth. This is the time to breathe and choose to see what others can see.

The Old Book

I burn the pages of the old, tattered book

Of all the lies that had haunted me for years.

No echo of them is left in my heart.

As I watch the destruction of the pages full of tears.

My Lord came and drew me close and spoke,

"Look and see. I have a new book to read for you".

He gave to me another brand new book.

Revealing every promise, every prophecy, and every truth.

I saw the poetry of love written over me,

The joyful lyrics and the stanzas drowning sorrows bringing peace.

I feast upon its pages, and the delights held within.

I request, "Lord, read some more for me!"

He laughs as my happiness delights Him.

I shine with His approval like a star in the sky!

He whispers over every barren part of me,

Dispelling every lie.

And now I stand complete in Him,

All accusations silenced by His roar.

I become who He always said I was

As in my identity, I soar.

THE CALLING THROUGH THE LOCK

Inspired by Song of Songs Chapter 4

I hear the whisper through the lock of my door

As you entreat me to open up to you, my King, and my Lord.

I tarry as I see the shadows within,

Fearing you will look with judging eyes, calling them 'sin'.

And yet, you call me "Flawless, Beauty divine"

And speak of your desire for our hearts to entwine.

Your passionate plea melts away my resolve made in shame

As your melodic petition sings out my name.

I relinquish—overwhelmed, undone by your love

And unlock the places untouched by your love.

You speak of our union,

The love-covenant sealed by you, my King.

I release to you my shadows, as my whole heart, I bring.

You call me "Innocent, Beloved," revealing your heart.

I call you my God-Man, my King, yielding my inner parts.

Together we are undone, embraced in this pure love divine—

A dark yet lovely bride, restored to her King.

Spirit Man

I am spirit but I live in flesh.

I have my being in Him and in me He resides.

We are called 'jars of clay!'

For all the glory of my physical form,

It is my spirit that soars.

My spirit flies and dwells in heaven,

It meets with the Father and communes with the Son.

My feet stand on mud,

Yet my heart soars in heaven

While my spirit roars with angels and joins victory's song.

I am to be seen, interact, become weary and grow strong.

But my spirit, so ageless, pulls me up to the throne.

My eyes do not see it and my ears do not hear

But my spirit rejoices as she enjoys heaven's delights.

She calls me forth to be near,

Near to Him, the Eternal One,

The great I Am and the glorious Son.

'Sovereign Femininity' is a bold, feminine piece using strong colours and bold sweeps to depict passion, intimacy, and feminine strength. This strength comes from our surrender to Him, as well as understanding our identity in the Kingdom as women of God.

Royal Identity

Embracing sovereignty in our identity,

Understanding our restored royalty.

Loyalty to the sacrificed King,

The God-Man who gave it all to bring us back in.

And now we stand in the throne room,

Confident, righteous, holy, and whole.

Not trusting in religion or the works of the soul

But understanding we are the bride, betrothed to the Son.

We run over the mountains alongside the One

Who redeems all to Himself as we answer His call,

And we, His sovereign bride, surrender our all.

"...if anyone is in Christ, he is a new creation. The old has passed away; behold, the new has come."

2 Corinthians 5:17 (ESV)

Part Three

The Intimate Poet

Foreword

This final section is devoted to my poetry of passion. It testifies to my love and adoration of King Jesus and the intimate relationship we share together.

It is uniquely personal to me and demonstrates how my heart and soul respond to the pursuit of the love He has lavished on me.

It is not about my head knowledge of an Almighty God but an internal conversation from my heart to His and His to mine.

It is the fire within that motivates my whole life.

'Hearts Collide' was my response to an encounter I had with God, where I sensed Him pull at my heart and it felt as if it literally collided into His. It represents the love exchange as hearts meet in mutual love.

*H*earts *C*ollide

I sit on the inside and look up to see His face,

His magnetic heart pulls my heart into His embrace.

I don't resist as I feel my heart fly up to Him

And I understand that now I am resting within

The walls of the heart of my Bridegroom King.

I expand as I diminish—as I become lowly, so I grow.

I stand inside of my Creator God as I let my heart go.

I am on a collision course to meet the heart of God

As I sit down on the inside at the feet of my Lord.

ENTANGLED

Spirits intertwined,

I'm entangled in you.

My being infused, interwoven with the essence of you.

Living as one in perfect symmetry,

Inseparable union as you dwell within me.

You roared as you leapt over the mountains to awaken my heart.

The same voice that brought creation, called forth my inner parts.

My longings fulfilled in your sweet embrace,

Stoking the fire of desire as we meet face to face.

I throw off self.

I am no longer my own.

I yield to the truth; I am your beloved one.

Such sweet symphony, as entangled, we grow,

Your frequency calling out what was already known.

No more calling through the halls of my deserted soul

As we meet in the inner place together.

In our union, I'm whole.

The Chamber

His hand is on the latch,

And I catch my breath

As He whispers my name.

I release my grip on what I held so tightly

And I answer in reply to His sigh,

And He enters the dusty chamber of my heart.

What once was dark

Is full of light.

What was barren

Is full of life.

What once was dry

Is drowned in love.

He moves in this space that was empty,

Now it overflows.

The chamber of my heart

Is now His resting place.

My Gift

I bring my sacrifice wrapped in devotion.

I bring it all and lay it before the throne.

I take it to the altar to burn as an offering,

All of it, holding nothing back. All for the King.

The best of me—the great moments and every good deed,

Any righteousness accrued, pure and holy moments

Or meeting others' needs.

My praise and trophies, accolades and all my approval from man,

I unwrap it here and lay it down before the great I Am.

The filthy rags I offer you, you'll receive with fire.

Yet you have something better to bestow, it is your desire.

You lay a cloak around me and fill me till I overflow.

Your humility that you won for me shrouds me as I go.

My gift seems small and tacky,

Yours is shimmering bright.

You accept the exchange with gladness,

For I have given all for your light.

Now I wear this mantle with pure joy,

My sacrifice is done.

All I have and all I am, I give

In honour of the Son.

'I Kiss the Son' To come before God is terrifying, yet we are bold enough to kiss the face of God who became a man, and ultimately, our Bridegroom. This artwork has the stripes He carries upon His body, and also His blood, His holiness, and His glory.

*I K*iss the *S*on

Dare I kiss the cheek of the Most High God?

Dare I kiss the cheek that carried the tears for my lost soul—

My broken life, my wounded heart?

Dare I kiss the face of the Man who is God?

Dare I kiss the One who took the hit for my pain,

My hateful rebellion and crippling shame?

Dare I kiss the face of the Man who took mine?

Dare I kiss the Man who made mine His own?

My empty heart, my conditional love!

Dare I kiss the Son who is the King?

Dare I kiss the King of heaven,

Who reaches for me and whispers my name?

In the dark, I hear His voice.

In the light, I feel His glory!

So I kiss the Son, the Most High God.

I kiss my King, my own One

Who ravished my heart by loving me

When I hated all and said, "Not yet!".

(Continued....)

I kiss the face of the One who cried my tears.

I kiss the Man who cried out for my sin,

Who took what was mine and gave me His

While I was unaware, while I was in the dark.

He stands so close and I feel Him near.

I kiss the face of the Man who is GOD.

I KISS THE SON.

ENTWINED

I am choosing to live entwined,

His heartbeat sounding with mine.

Our fingers interlaced as His face shines,

As He rests His forehead on mine.

As one we sway to heaven's song

This is my home, where I belong.

I feel His embrace enfold me, so strong.

His countenance stirs my settled places

As we live here together face to face.

His radiant beauty filling all my spaces

I am content yet raptured

Peacefully passionate

And joyfully overwhelmed.

Every fragment and shattered part

Collected to become one with His heart

I am His work of art.

His light absorbs all of me.

Darkness flees the forgotten parts, and I am free

To become His dream, This is my destiny.

The tremors of trauma are silenced

As I become His sweet fragrance,

And continue to be held by His presence.

We live together entwined.

*L*ovesick

(Taken from 'The Company of Laid Down Lovers' J Gibbs 2021)

I was heartsick before when you called me back,

Away from the Liar and the noisy bustle of life.

You loved on me as you restored and healed all broken, jagged parts of my soul.

Your fiery, intense love burned within me

'Till the ashes revealed the beauty of you.

And now my identity is restored, and I am whole.

I am His and He is mine.

This love-exchange is real.

Not just a God-Man saving sinners

But a Lover-King wooing a bride.

I was heartsick and now I am lovesick.

A true bridal romance, where I have stolen His heart and He has mine.

So much more perfect than we can imagine.

The ultimate love, so pure and divine.

I want to stay in this lovesick moment,

To rest here and close the door.

The world has its delights but can no way compare

With this, this secret place.

This space where our love is exchanged,

Where I have ravished His heart too

So that He rides over the mountains singing my name.

The intense burning in His heart for me,

A pure, jealous love that roars

For every unsurrendered part of my heart,

For He is lovesick too!

Jane Gibbs

'Into the Mist' **is** our desire to step into the presence of God. The air is fresh and the light is bright. We love this private and holy ground, even though we cannot see far ahead.

Secret Place

My heart is captivated by your gaze,

I am strong as I stand in praise

At the doorway of our secret place.

As you turn to me with your beautiful face.

My heart beats violently in my chest

And I edge forward to enter the rest.

I look neither left nor right,

I am entranced by the sight of you, my King.

My everything.

My heart is always yours.

I walk in and close the door.

It's you and I in intimacy,

The secret place where I am free

To pour my fragrant offering

Upon the feet of my Holy King.

My life, my heart, my whole, my breath.

I lay down my crown and lay on your chest.

SWEET BLISS

Sweet joy fills me up and I rest.

I laugh and smile, for I am blessed.

He sings sweet music for my heart to possess.

I sing sweet worship with all my breath.

So our duet is poetry, music, and song,

For the bride and the Bridegroom, together, belong.

He dies and she lives, and victory is won.

Surrender, a weapon, and the death of a Son.

A cross, the symbol of love; sweet death is bliss.

And she is awoken by love's sweet kiss.

My eyes are now open and I see the King.

Our passionate duet, forever, we sing.

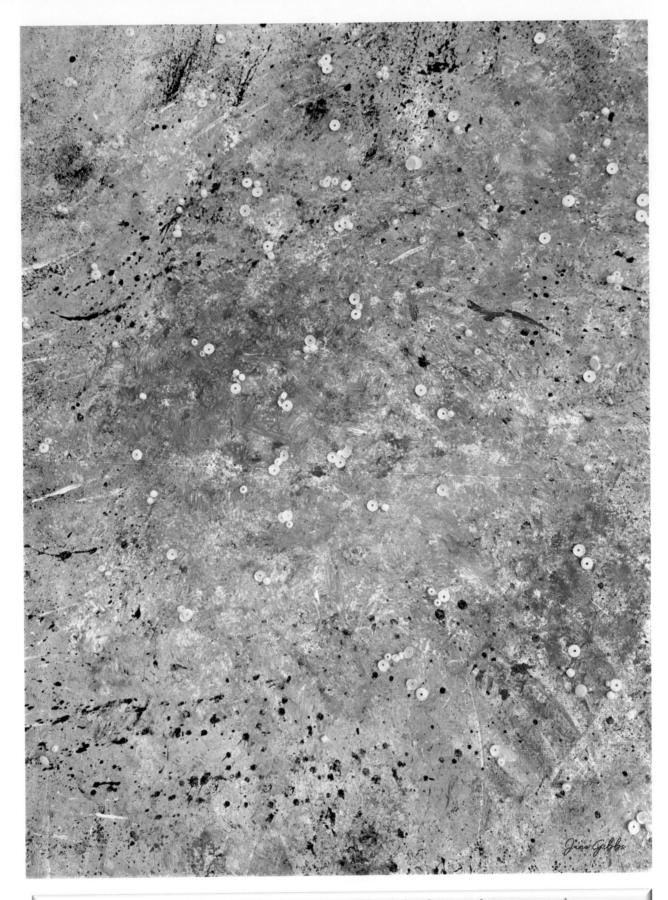

'Bridal Love' sings through the pastel colours of feminine love and represents the romantic love the bride (the Church) has for Christ. It is both bridal and royal in its colour and texture.

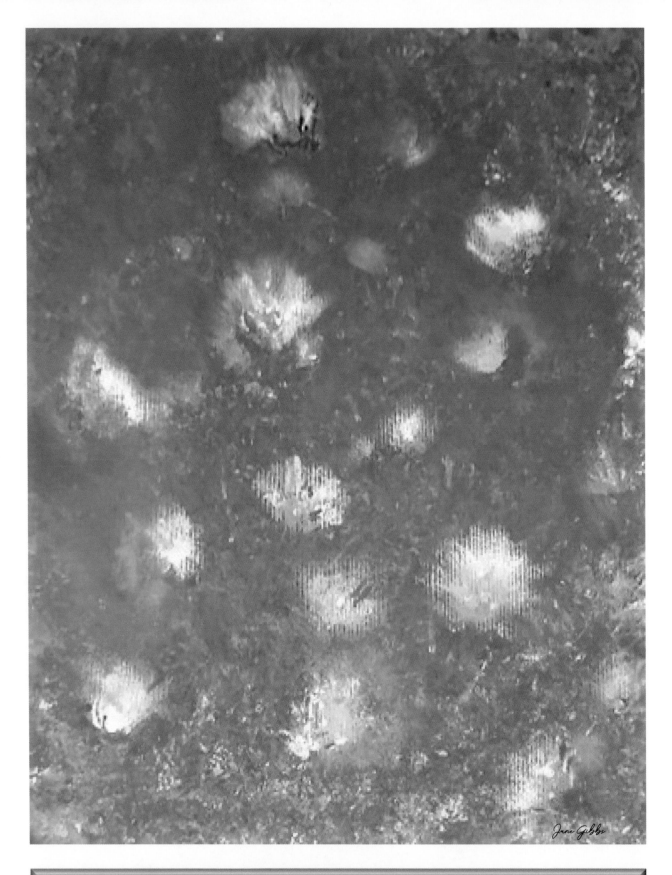

'Encounters in the Secret Place' The dark shrubbery background is indicative of the secret place of our private oneness with the Lord. The flashes of pink and white flowers demonstrate intimacy met by the Holy Spirit, which leads to encountering Jesus in this most private and precious place; our innermost heart of hearts.

The Garden

This place, this space,

Set apart for me—so wild, so free.

To others it looks less ordered

But it's our place, our space.

It's where you come to encounter me.

It's you and I in this secret hideaway.

My fragrance inviting you in,

Enticing the heart of you, my King.

It's where I go to encounter you.

We go to love, to laugh, to dance.

We meet each other here together, this divine romance.

It's yours—unique to you. You love it that way.

It's my created heart, made in your image, on display.

To display your wonders, to reveal your face,

To show the world your amazing grace.

Behind my face, the image of you,

In who I am, not what I do.

I meet you here, invitation received,

To play and be loved; wholly free.

I run to this garden, to my love that is true,

To be who I am, made complete in you.

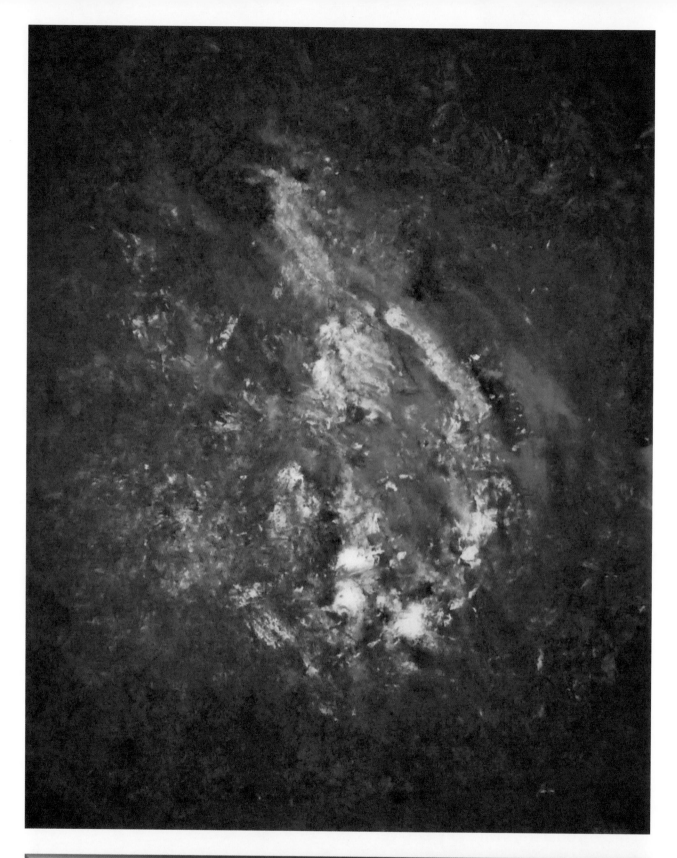

'Indwelling Intimacy (The Space)' This was a prophetic word I received in August 2019 which I won't repeat in full here but explains how the Holy Spirit would meet God's people in the secret place. It symbolises the birthing and creating of something. It is the beginning of creation where God spoke into the space and created the cosmos.

Your Face

To see your face,

Just a glimpse is enough.

I have dove's eyes,

A pursuit of the One my heart loves.

I am yours and I am undone.

All this world offers could never satisfy.

To see your face and yours alone;

My deepest longing, my desire.

Where darkness flees and glory shines,

No other beauty to compare,

For I see your face.

About the Author

Jane Gibbs is a contemporary Christian artist living in the West Country in the UK. She has spent her adult life pursuing and being pursued by Jesus, the Lover of her soul. In her creativity she longs to show the heart of God to others, carrying the authentic, raw, and undiluted love of Jesus.

As one of the Founding Members of the Liz Wright International Mentoring Community, Jane strives to encourage the collective pursuit of surrendered love to Jesus, which is the passionate and intimate journey of His beloved bride. She champions others to understand their beautiful identity in Him.

If you are interested to learn more about my work, to purchase a print of any of the artwork found in this book, or indeed wish to look at other pieces of my art, please contact me at jgibbscreative@btinternet.com

Follow and connect with me:

Facebook Page: @Janegibbscreative

Public Facebook Group: @Janegibbscreative

Instagram: @janegibbscreative

The Company of Laid Down Lovers is Jane Gibbs' first book published in 2021.

"It is an invitation to journey with Him and reach His heart with ours. It begins with a call and a wooing: it becomes a connection. It's a journey of intimacy and the destination is friendship with God."

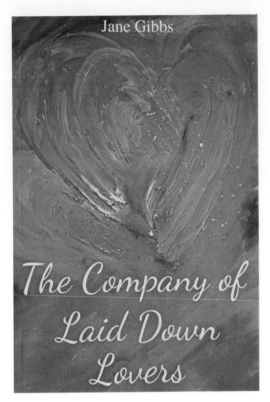

What others are saying about The Company of Laid Down Lovers:

Amazon reviews:

"Jane writes with an honesty and depth that draws you into her journey with Jesus and leaves an impression upon your heart. I felt the authenticity of a life laid down before Jesus, the dive into the waters of His love, The letting go of all else but Him."

"It's about the journey of finding the relationship of perfect union we were created to have with Father, Jesus, and Holy Spirit, and about living in a place of rest and encounter. It is full of great nuggets of truth, is very real, and leaves the reader passionate to go deeper."

The Company of Laid Down Lovers is available in paperback and as an eBook on Amazon.com.

Also coming in 2023 Jane Gibbs' 12 week devotional which will be available through Amazon in paperback and eBook.

Printed in Great Britain
by Amazon

15881750R00054